Braving
the
Frozen
Frontier

Braving
the
Frozen
Frontier

Women Working in Antarctica

Rebecca L. Johnson

Lerner Publications Company

Minneapolis

In memory of my mother,
who has always guided me toward the light

With support through the National Science Foundation's Antarctic Artists and Writers Program, I have twice had the privilege of visiting Antarctica. This book is based on my personal interactions with some of the many women I met during my time on the continent.

I want to thank all those women who agreed to be interviewed, who invited me to their work sites and field camps, often for extended periods of time, and who so freely shared with me their experiences and impressions of what it is like to work and live on the Ice.

Many thanks, too, to the members of NSF's Office of Polar Programs, and to the civilian and military support groups in Antarctica who provided me with first-rate survival training, outstanding logistics support, and enthusiastic assistance always. Finally, I want to thank Lucia de Leiris and Jody Forster for their special effort in helping with photographs.

Library of Congress Cataloging-in-Publication Data
Johnson, Rebecca L.
    Braving the frozen frontier : women working in Antarctica / by Rebecca L. Johnson.
       p.   cm.
    Includes bibliographical references and index.
    Summary: Describes the day-to-day experiences of several women who work as scientists, helicopter pilots, snowplow drivers, and doctors in Antarctica.
    ISBN 0-8225-2855-X (alk. paper)
    1. Antarctica—Discovery and exploration—Juvenile literature. 2. Women explorers— Juvenile literature. 3. Women scientists—Juvenile literature. [1. Antarctica—Discovery and exploration. 2. Explorers. 3. Scientists. 4. Women—Biography.] I. Title.
    G860.J64   1997
    919.8'904—dc20   96–13972

Manufactured in the United States of America
1 2 3 4 5 6 – JR – 02 01 00 99 98 97

Contents

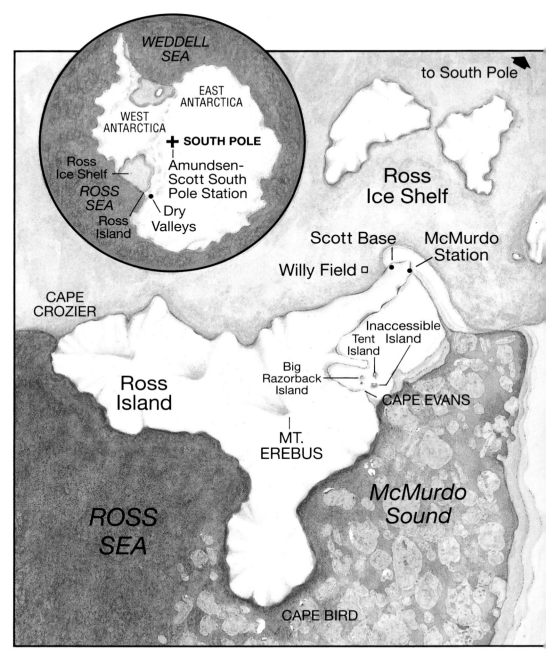

to South Pole

WEDDELL SEA

EAST ANTARCTICA

WEST ANTARCTICA

+ SOUTH POLE

Amundsen-Scott South Pole Station

Ross Ice Shelf

ROSS SEA

Ross Island

Dry Valleys

Ross Ice Shelf

Scott Base

McMurdo Station

Willy Field □

CAPE CROZIER

Inaccessible Island

Tent Island

Big Razorback Island

Ross Island

CAPE EVANS

MT. EREBUS

McMurdo Sound

ROSS SEA

CAPE BIRD

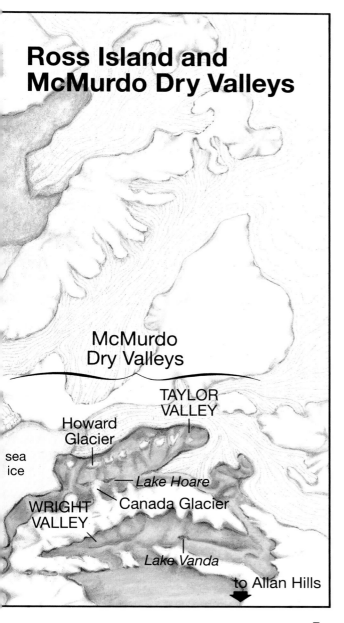

Ross Island and McMurdo Dry Valleys

McMurdo
Dry Valleys

TAYLOR
VALLEY

Howard
Glacier

sea
ice

Lake Hoare

WRIGHT
VALLEY

Canada Glacier

Lake Vanda

to Allan Hills

Ross Island lies just off the coast of Antarctica at about 78° south latitude. McMurdo Station, located on the southernmost point of the island, is the largest scientific research outpost in Antarctica. The station is the base of operations for dozens of science teams that do research at far-flung sites around Ross Island and on the continent.

1

To the Ice Edge

Lieutenant Judy Coffman tightened her grip on the controls of *Gentle 16* as a savage gust of wind made the helicopter shudder and swerve. Three hundred feet below, slithering ribbons of blowing snow raced across the sea's frozen surface. Driven by the fiercely cold Antarctic wind, these "snow snakes" and the helicopter were headed toward the same place—the ice edge, where the sea ice of McMurdo Sound meets the open waters of the Ross Sea.

It was mid-October, spring in Antarctica. Gray clouds hung low in the sky. The temperature outside was a numbing twenty degrees below zero. It wasn't all that much warmer inside the helicopter. Ice crystals trimmed the window edges, and every metal surface in the cockpit radiated waves of cold.

Like her copilot, Lieutenant Adam Paterson, seated next to her in the cockpit, Judy was dressed from head to toe in olive green, extreme cold weather clothing, from the thickly insulated mukluks on her feet to her bulky flight suit and jacket. An embroidered patch on Judy's flight suit showed a frosty skull and crossbones centered over outspread wings—the symbol of the Ice Pirates, the U.S. Navy's Antarctic helicopter squadron.

Stretching out from the Antarctic coast, the sea ice meets the waters of the open sea.

*Judy Coffman, at
the controls*

Judy was one of twelve pilots providing helicopter support for
the United States Antarctic Program that season—and the first
female helicopter pilot in the squadron's history.

Antarctica is one of the last wild places on earth. It is a huge
continent, shrouded in ice, home to blizzards and icebergs and
penguins. Every spring, dozens of scientists working with the
U.S. Antarctic Program arrive on the continent to learn more
about this vast white wilderness at the bottom of the world.
Many of these scientists are based at McMurdo Station, the
program's largest research outpost. McMurdo is located on
Ross Island, which is separated from the Antarctic mainland by
McMurdo Sound. Judy's job was to fly people and cargo to and
from study sites, field camps, and other destinations within a
two-hundred-mile radius of McMurdo Station.

Judy glanced over her shoulder at the passengers in the back
of the helicopter. Diane Stoecker, Jeff Merrell, and Dan
Gustafson were crammed together on the single bench seat between two crew members. Nearly buried under equipment and

survival gear, the three scientists were trying to balance a long sled on their knees. "How are y'all doing back there?" Judy asked in her faint Texas drawl. She spoke into the small microphone attached to her helmet. It was hooked into the helicopter's internal communication system, or ICS. Everyone aboard was on the ICS. It was the only way to be heard above the roar of the engines and the rotor whirling overhead.

"We're squashed, but fine," Diane replied with a laugh. "We need about three hours of ground time at the edge to get everything done, Judy. Think that'll be possible today?"

"That depends on what the weather decides to do," said Judy. "If it doesn't get any worse than this—no problem. But if the weather gods get angry, we'll have to pull out sooner than that. No one wants to camp out down there!" She gave a nod to the windswept ice below.

Another gust of wind rocked the helicopter, and Judy turned her attention back to flying. During her first year in Antarctica, she'd flown strictly as a copilot, training in the cockpit beside more seasoned pilots. In her second year she'd become a full-fledged polar aircraft commander. This year, her third season, Judy was still enjoying flying where good weather could deteriorate into a raging blizzard in less than an hour. She was even getting used to the cold.

Patches of blue were appearing in the clouds overhead—the weather seemed to be improving. But Judy knew from experience that they might be flying into what she and the other pilots called a sucker hole—a temporary clearing in the weather that could close in again unbelievably fast. She squinted through the dark visor on her helmet. A faint gray line was visible on the horizon where the ice abruptly ended and the open ocean began.

Alone in a world of blue and white, a helicopter flies over the sea ice.

Ten minutes later, the ice edge was almost directly beneath them. Judy eased the helicopter into a tight banking turn and flew along the border between ice and water, looking for a good place to land. She circled slowly over a promising spot about two hundred yards from the edge. The horizon tilted dizzyingly as the helicopter soared around in a great arc above the glittering icescape.

Judy brought the helicopter around to face into the wind and began the final approach to landing. A hundred and fifty feet above the ice, a crew member pulled open the right rear door, leaned far out for a clear view of the surface below, and started guiding Judy down through the descent. "Easy down," he said as they neared the ice. "Six feet. Easy down. Steady.

Three feet. Two. Six inches. Heels down. Toes down. Good four-point."

The runners of the helicopter were resting lightly on the frozen surface of the sea, but Judy wouldn't let the full weight of the aircraft down onto the ice until she knew it was thick enough to support them. The water below the ice was several thousand feet deep. With the main rotor whirling over his head, the crew member climbed out of the helicopter and stepped gingerly down onto the slippery surface. He grabbed a hand-operated drill and began drilling into the ice at his feet. Through the open door, Diane watched as the long drill bit gradually disappeared. "Looks good, Lieutenant—it's more than three feet thick," the crewman announced over the ICS.

"Roger," Judy replied, as she let the helicopter settle firmly onto the ice and began shutting down its engines. The throbbing whine of the rotor died away as it gradually slowed to a stop. An eerie silence followed, broken only by the sound of the wind and the hiss of blowing snow hitting the windows. They were down among the snow snakes, and the wild wind was sucking the last traces of warmth out of the helicopter.

While the crew tied the main rotor down to keep it from spinning in the wind, Adam radioed back to McMurdo Station to report their position, adding that *Gentle 16* would be "on deck" for three hours, weather permitting. Diane eased the sled out the open door, extracted her stiff legs from the gear piled around her feet, and climbed out of the helicopter. The vicious wind brought tears to her eyes that froze instantly on her eyelashes. She looked down at the ice. It was hard to believe she was standing on the frozen surface of the sea.

It was also hard to grasp just how much sea ice there is around Antarctica. Every March, as winter descends on the continent, the sea's surface begins to freeze, and sea ice forms at the incredible rate of twenty-two square miles a minute. By winter's end, the belt of sea ice ringing the continent covers roughly 7,500,000 square miles, an area nearly twice the size of the United States.

This was Diane's third season doing research in Antarctica. A biologist from the University of Maryland's Horn Point Environmental Laboratory, she specialized in studying algae and protozoa—single-celled organisms that are part of the ocean's plankton. The algae Diane was studying in Antarctica, however, live *inside* the sea ice much of the year.

Diane Stoecker collects samples of very salty water, or brine, from the sea ice.

As sea ice forms each winter, some planktonic algae become trapped inside. These ice-bound algae survive, however, because sea ice is honeycombed with small interconnected passageways. The passageways, called brine channels, contain very salty water—at least six times saltier than seawater. Some types of algae not only survive, but thrive, in brine channels.

When the sea ice begins to melt in the spring, the brine channels enlarge to form small chambers, like miniature aquariums, where the algae grow and multiply. As the ice continues to melt, countless numbers of algae are released into the water to join the rest of the plankton.

Diane was fascinated by sea-ice algae. She was here with Jeff, her graduate student, and Dan, her lab technician, to study the algae, and answer questions about them. For example: What are conditions like inside brine channels? What are the different stages in the life cycles of sea-ice algae, and when do they occur? When the algae are locked up in the ice, where do they get all the nutrients they need to survive? Once released back into the water, how important are these tiny plant-like organisms in the Antarctic food web?

"Jeff, let's you and I load the Niskin bottle and the other water sampling gear into the sled," Diane said, as she pulled the sled alongside the open helicopter door.

"I'll get started coring," Dan added, opening the box that contained a heavy ice corer. He carried the corer over to a spot some distance from the helicopter and began screwing it down into the ice. He hoped that the long cylinders of ice he'd cut out with the corer would be full of algae.

Jeff looped the tow rope of the loaded sled over his shoulder and took the ice ax Diane handed him. Pulling her neck gaiter up to protect her nose and cheeks from the wind, Diane took a

Jeff Merrell and Diane prepare a Niskin bottle to take sea water samples at the ice edge.

firm grip on her own ice ax and set out across the sea ice. She and Jeff bent into the wind as they headed for the ice edge.

Tap, tap, tap-tap-tap. The sound of axes striking ice rang through the air as Jeff and Diane tested spots where the sea ice looked cracked before crossing them. As they neared the edge of the ice and the open water, Diane could feel her heart begin to beat a little faster. The ice edge can be a dangerous place. Leopard seals often patrol its length, looking for penguins to snatch off the ice and eat. From experience, Diane knew that leopard seals will sometimes try this with people too. The year before, one of her graduate students had been grabbed by a leopard seal at the ice edge and almost pulled into the water.

This year Diane was taking no chances. She and Jeff stopped about twenty feet from the open water, and while Jeff drove a long sturdy ice screw into the ice, Diane struggled into a safety harness and cinched it tightly around her waist. Then she attached one end of a rope to the ice screw and threaded the

Diane struggles into her safety harness.

other end through her harness. She was securely anchored to the ice. If a leopard seal attacked while she was working at the edge and managed to pull her into the frigid water, Jeff could use the rope to yank her back to safety.

Diane picked up the Niskin bottle, a long tubular instrument used to collect water samples at various depths. She wanted to find out if the algae that live in the brine channels of the ice were also present in the open water at this time of year. The samples she was going to get today would help her determine that. Diane cautiously approached the water. Waves lapped the edge of the ice, making it treacherously slippery. She lowered the Niskin bottle into the dark water for the first sample. As she hauled it back up, she heard Jeff shout "LOOK OUT!" A black shape surfaced for a split second farther out in the water.

Briefly airborne, an emperor penguin soars out of the sea.

Diane quickly stepped back, expecting a leopard seal. But to her surprise and delight, an emperor penguin came exploding out of the sea to land on the ice. Swaying slightly from side to side, the big bird walked right up to Diane. It stood as high as her waist. For several seconds, scientist and penguin simply stared at each other. Diane smiled. In Antarctica, animals show little fear of people, just enormous curiosity.

"Here come some more!" called Jeff, and two more emperors came leaping up onto the ice. This pair seemed more interested in the contents of the sled than in the scientists. While Diane and Jeff finished collecting the water samples, the penguins circled the sled, peering into pails and boxes and poking

An audience of emperor penguins

around in the other gear with their sharp beaks. Every few minutes, another penguin would pop up out of the sea. By the time the scientists headed back to the helicopter, their feathered audience numbered nearly a dozen.

Dan was just starting on the last core when Diane and Jeff returned. Three people working together made the job go quickly. Ten minutes later, the samples of ice and water had been loaded aboard the helicopter, and the scientists were strapping themselves in for the flight back to McMurdo. The crew released the main rotor and climbed aboard as Judy started up the engines. The cold metal blades turned reluctantly at first, then faster and faster as the helicopter came roaring to life. Pilot and copilot ran through their checklists for takeoff. "Gages are green, power is good," said Judy. She brought the helicopter up into a hover and then soared off across the ice, gaining speed and climbing to five hundred feet in a matter of seconds. She followed familiar landmarks along the coastline of Ross Island until the dark volcanic hills that surround McMurdo Station came into view.

Judy got on the radio with Mac Center, McMurdo's version of air traffic control: "Mac Center, this is *Gentle One-Six.*"

"*One-Six,* go ahead," came the response. Judy relayed their position. In return she got an update on the wind speed and direction and was given clearance to land. McMurdo Station, a cluster of brown and gray buildings connected by a few winding gravel tracks, was below them. Moments later, Judy brought the helicopter gently down to earth on the station's helicopter pad.

Diane and her team scrambled to unload their equipment and samples and pile everything into the back of a waiting pickup truck. With a wave of thanks to the pilots and crew, they were driven off to the Crary Lab, McMurdo's sprawling science center. There they would melt the samples of sea ice to release the algae living in it and filter the samples of seawater to see what they contained.

McMurdo Station on Ross Island

On the helicopter pad, Judy stretched in her seat and wiggled her fingers to drive out the cold. Her next group of passengers—a science team going across the sound into the mountains on the continent—was ready and waiting to get on board. As soon as *Gentle 16* was refueled, Judy and her crew would be airborne again.

———————— ⑅ ————————

At first glance, the fact that women fly helicopters and head science teams in Antarctica might not seem remarkable or even unusual. But it wasn't always that way.

For nearly 150 years after men first set foot on the southern-most continent in 1821, Antarctica was truly a man's world, discovered, explored, and inhabited by men. During that time, women were rare visitors to Antarctica. In the 1960s, however, the situation began to change, and in 1969 the first female participants in the U.S. Antarctic Program arrived on the continent. Christine Muller-Schwarze, a psychologist, came to study penguins on Ross Island with her zoologist husband. Lois Jones, a geochemist, headed a four-woman geology team that did research in a remote field camp, far from McMurdo Station.

Judy stands by her helicopter on McMurdo's helo pad.

Every year, many women experience the challenge of working in Antarctica.

These Antarctic pioneers paved the way for many other women to take part in polar research.

In the 1990s, women are well-represented in the U.S. Antarctic Program and in the research programs of several other countries. In addition to dozens of female scientists, there are women doing almost every kind of job imaginable in Antarctica. Women work as electricians, carpenters, construction supervisors, lab technicians, shuttle drivers, cooks, pilots, heavy equipment operators, meteorologists, cargo handlers, and computer specialists. Every season there are newcomers, in addition to the old hands who return year after year.

Many of the women in Antarctica, like the men they work alongside, are drawn to the continent by the opportunities for scientific discovery and the chance to experience one of the most unspoiled and challenging environments on earth.

A snow-covered Weddell seal and her pup laze on the sea ice after a blizzard.

2

Whiteout

Sarah Krall moved purposefully down the narrow aisles in the Food Room, singing along with the bluegrass music that blared from the stereo on her desk. The odors of spices, coffee, and tea filled the air around her as she scanned the tall wooden shelves. Her gaze settled on a shelf piled with bulging bags of cashews and walnuts, dates and raisins and dried apricots. Sarah ran a slim finger down the list she carried, talking to herself between bursts of song: "Dates . . . nope. Figs . . . three." She grabbed three bags of plump dried figs and then stepped over to a shelf where dozens of big Cadbury chocolate bars lay in neat, fragrant stacks. Sarah glanced at the list again: "Chocolate bars . . . ten almond, ten Dairy Milk, ten Fruit and Nut, and five peppermint." She counted out the bars and carried the load of chocolate and figs to the middle of the room, where several boxes stood open on the worn wooden floor. She added the dried fruit and candy to the packets and cartons and bags of food the boxes already contained. Tomorrow, weather permitting, these boxes of food would be accompanying a team of scientists out to a remote region of the continent.

The Food Room is a strange sort of grocery store, tucked away on the second floor of one of McMurdo's older buildings. Long rows of shelves packed with food run the length of the room. They hold everything that anyone planning a trip into

Sarah Krall, at work in McMurdo's Food Room

the wilds of Antarctica might want, from dried beans and pasta, canned stew and soups, to trail mix and, of course, chocolate bars. In Antarctica, chocolate is a necessity.

Sarah was in charge of the Food Room. It was her job to help scientists plan their food requirements for life in the field and supply them with what they needed, whether they were going to be away from the station for a few days or a few months. More than fifty thousand pounds of food passed through the Food Room each season. Almost singlehandedly, Sarah organized and distributed all of it.

Sarah flipped back through the list, checking to see what sorts of freeze-dried and dehydrated foods this group of scientists had requested. It was important that the types of food scientists took into the field suited not just their tastes, but their habits too. This group was going to be on the move most of the time, traveling by snowmobile and towing their supplies behind them on sleds. Keeping weight to a minimum was essential, so lightweight, dehydrated foods were a good choice. Heavier supplies, like canned goods, were fine for science teams that didn't move around as much and could handle the extra weight, along with the extra cooking equipment and fuel it took to make more elaborate meals.

Alongside the chocolate bars that lay nestled in the boxes were bags of nuts and trail mix and granola bars, packets of hot cocoa, and tins of smoked oysters and peach preserves. In this land of blizzards and subzero temperatures, high-calorie, high-fat foods were a normal part of life. People needed lots of calories in their diet just to stay warm.

A skilled mountaineer and wilderness survival expert, Sarah knew from experience that in a harsh environment like Antarctica food wasn't just a source of calories. It was a source of comfort too. After a long day of working in the snow and wind and cold, she knew what it felt like to retreat to the snug safety of a tent, devour a plate of steaming hot food, and then sit back with a full stomach and enjoy the sensation of tense muscles relaxing, cold toes thawing, and her entire body . . . getting . . . really . . . warm!

Back in the early days of Antarctic exploration, the men who traveled to remote parts of the continent, far away from their expedition's main camp, had a very limited diet. For these early explorers, breakfast, lunch, and dinner usually consisted of crackers, a mixture of meat and fat called pemmican, butter, sugar, cocoa, and tea. The food supplies that Antarctic scientists now take into the field are varied, nutritionally balanced, and easy to prepare. In many cases, making a hot meal is as easy as adding boiling water to a package of freeze-dried food.

Sarah surveyed the boxes at her feet and checked their contents against the list one more time. Everything was accounted for, except a few items of frozen food. Those she would add to the boxes just before the scientists left the station. With a satisfied smile, she sat down at her desk, cranked up the music, and began to study the food list for another science group. She enjoyed outfitting science teams with food, calculating weights and portions and calories, and coming up with creative ways to satisfy the food cravings that people often get when they are far from home in a strange and inhospitable place.

Over the pounding beat of the music, Sarah heard heavy boots on the stairs. The door burst open, and two women in red parkas stomped in. "Hey, Sarah!" called Jennifer Moss. "We just happened to be in town and thought we'd stop by."

Jenn's companion, Tania Zenteno-Savin, tossed her hood back and peeled off her mittens. She gave Sarah a hopeful look. "I'm dying for some real Mexican food and promised I'd cook out at camp. Have you got any tortillas?"

Jenn and Tania were part of S-004, a team of scientists who had a field camp on the sea ice about fifteen miles north of Mc-Murdo at the base of Big Razorback Island. These researchers were studying Weddell seals in McMurdo Sound, a fact that had earned their group the nickname "Seal Heads" around the station. Jenn and Tania were graduate students from the University of Alaska in Fairbanks, where they were both working on Ph.D.'s in marine mammal biology. This was Tania's first season studying seals in Antarctica. It was Jenn's second.

The members of S-004 usually came into town each weekend to pick up supplies, wash their clothes, and take showers. But an urgent errand had brought Jenn and Tania in at midweek, and before they headed back to camp, they wanted to see what

Jennifer Moss (standing) *and Tania Zenteno-Savin, with a playful young Weddell seal*

treats Sarah might have on hand. They left the Food Room with flour tortillas, onions, and a dozen fresh oranges.

The two women walked down through McMurdo and out onto the sea ice where they had parked their snowmobiles. Tania stowed the food in the big survival bag that was strapped to her machine. Inside the bag were a tent, a tiny stove and fuel, packets of freeze-dried food, a shovel, maps, and other items that might come in handy—and quite possibly save their lives— if they happened to get stranded out on the ice. In addition to the big survival bag, Tania and Jenn each carried a smaller bag stuffed with extra warm clothes, snacks, and an insulated bottle of water. Carrying survival gear quickly becomes a way of life in Antarctica—no one ever leaves "home" without it.

Jenn straddled the cold seat of her snowmobile and pulled out a handheld radio from an inside pocket of her parka. "Mac Ops, Mac Ops, this Sierra-Zero-Zero-Four."

"Go ahead, Sierra-Zero-Zero-Four," answered a radio operator in McMurdo's field communications center.

"Mac Ops, two souls, Moss and Zenteno-Savin, are returning to Big Razorback. Estimated time of arrival," Jenn glanced at her watch, "thirteen hundred hours."

"Roger that. Have a safe trip." Mac Ops kept careful track of everyone who was traveling on the sea ice. The ice was riddled with cracks in places. Although safe routes were marked with flags, it was still a dangerous place to travel.

Jenn stowed her radio, pulled on her goggles, and drew burly windproof mitts over her gloves. She turned the key in the ignition. Her cold snowmobile sputtered reluctantly, then started up with a roar. "Ready?" she shouted over to Tania, who nodded and took the lead as they sped away across the ice along a flagged route that followed the rugged coast of Ross Island.

It was a fiercely cold way to travel, exposed to the bitter wind. But it wasn't long before Big Razorback and neighboring Tent and Inaccessible Islands appeared on the horizon. Compared to massive, mountainous Ross Island, these tiny outcroppings of volcanic rock were no more than jagged black streaks jutting up through the sea ice. Thirty minutes later, Tania and Jenn zoomed into camp. They strode up to the door of the main hut, kicked the snow from their boots, and stepped eagerly into the warmth.

The one-room hut smelled of fresh coffee, burnt toast, and wet socks. Kelly Hastings, another University of Alaska student,

The sun lights up the base of Big Razorback Island and the summit of Mount Erebus, beyond.

was pouring hot cocoa into a thermos. "What did you bring us?" she asked and smiled at the sight of the oranges.

The other two members of S-004 were sitting at the table, stuffing backpacks with beef jerky and granola bars. Tom Gelatt and Rob Jensen were graduate students from the University of Minnesota. "We're just about done making up the lunch bags," Tom said to Tania and Jenn. "When you guys have thawed out, we'll be ready to go."

Jenn poured herself a cup of cocoa. "Why don't you and Kelly do the seals down at Hutton Cliffs," she replied. "Rob and Tania and I can check out the colonies at Tent and Inaccessible."

For more than twenty years, scientists have been studying the Weddell seals in McMurdo Sound. This healthy, thriving population is one of the best-studied groups of seals in the world.

A Weddell mother and pup bask in the sun.

What researchers know about Weddell seals is helping them to better understand other seal species. Seal populations in the Northern Hemisphere are shrinking dramatically, and no one knows why. Scientists hope that the research being done on seals in Antarctica will provide them with clues to what is wrong with the seals in the North.

The "Seal Heads" at Big Razorback were investigating a variety of things about Weddell seals. Jenn was especially interested in how young seals learn to dive and how their bodies change as they grow from pups into adults. Tania was investigating seal hormones and blood chemistry. Kelly, Rob, and Tom were studying survival rates and the size of the seal population. Although the young scientists each had their own individual research projects, they worked together in the field.

By the time Jenn and Tania had changed into dry socks and hung their wet socks above the stove to dry, the others had loaded the snowmobiles with everything needed for a day of fieldwork. Kelly and Tom drove off toward several seal colonies along Ross Island's coast. Jenn, Tania, and Rob made for nearby Tent Island.

They could see the seals from a mile away, dark torpedo shapes stretched out on the ice. Every spring, the female Weddell seals that live in McMurdo Sound come up onto the ice to give birth to their pups. The scientists had to tag each newborn seal, and each year there were hundreds of newborns.

Jenn kneels beside one of her neighbors at Big Razorback.

The scientists parked their snowmobiles some distance from the colony and approached the seals on foot. Starting at one end of the colony, Jenn, Tania, and Rob searched for seals that needed to be tagged. The first candidate was a fluffy brown pup that looked to be about two days old. While Tania kept the mother seal at bay with gentle taps of a bamboo pole—and talked to her reassuringly in Spanish—Jenn attached a numbered plastic tag to one of the pup's rear flippers. The whole procedure took less than a minute. By the time Jenn had finished logging the tag numbers on her handheld computer, mother and pup were back together, nuzzling each other.

For several hours, the scientists worked their way through the colony, picking a careful path through tumbled blocks of broken ice and over snow-covered cracks. By the time they

Jenn tags a newborn Weddell seal while Tania distracts its mother.

After tagging, the
pup is measured.

reached the far end of the colony, they had tagged eight more pups. Cold, tired, and hungry, they trudged back to the snowmobiles, ready for a snack and something hot to drink. The wind had picked up while they had been tagging, but all of a sudden they noticed just how much the weather had changed. The nearby islands were still visible, but the wind was creating a ground blizzard. All around them the sea ice was gradually disappearing beneath a thick layer of blowing snow.

Rob suggested that they head for home. "If it gets much worse, we'll be stuck out here," he said. No one wanted to end up huddled in the lightweight tents that were packed in the survival bags, waiting for a storm to pass. Blizzards often last for days in Antarctica. They drove back to camp as fast as they dared.

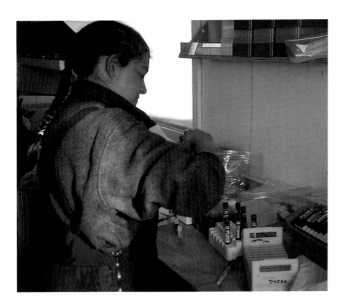

Tania analyzes seal blood samples in the lab at Big Razorback.

Tom and Kelly were already there, and their news about the weather wasn't good. A blizzard was bearing down on them from the south, and it looked like a big one. By eight o'clock, they had cleaned up the tagging gear, analyzed some seal blood samples, downloaded the data from their handheld computers to a laptop, and tied down everything around camp that could blow away.

The storm hit an hour later, as they were all sitting down to Tania's Mexican dinner of *enfrijoladas,* mole, and hot chocolate. The wind rose first to a moan and then a howl as it drove snow across the ice with savage fury. It struck the hut with such force that the little wooden building creaked and shuddered under the strain. Big Razorback Island disappeared behind a veil of blowing snow. So did everything else.

The storm raged all night, and in the morning snow was still blowing horizontally past the windows of the hut. But by late afternoon, the wind seemed to die down a bit. Jenn scraped the frost off a window and peered out. "I can see . . . six flags in a row on the route leading up to camp. Maybe it's letting up." She and the others were anxious to get back to work. The research season was short, and this storm had already cost them an entire day.

Another hour passed. The visibility was still too limited for snowmobile travel, but Jenn thought it would be safe to venture out in the Spryte, their slow-moving tracked vehicle. She needed to collect seal droppings to study Weddell seal diets, and she knew there was a good chance of finding those at Cape Evans, about five miles north of Big Razorback. With luck, she and Tania could drive there along the flagged route, collect what they needed, and be back in two hours.

The two women dressed in their warmest clothes and piled their survival bags into the back of the Spryte. The cold vehicle coughed to life, and they started off along the flagged route. The wind-driven snow still blotted out the surface of the ice, but Jenn and Tania could always see three or four flags in a row. The Spryte chugged jerkily along while the windshield wipers beat out a rhythmic slap, slap, slap.

All went well until they reached Cape Evans and saw what the storm had done. Any seal droppings that might have been on the shore were buried under several feet of drifted snow. There was nothing to do but turn around and go back.

Jenn spun the Spryte around on the ice and began following the flags back. On the way out, the wind had been behind them. Now they were driving directly into it. After they had traveled only a few hundred feet, Jenn brought the Spryte to a jerking stop.

"Tania," she said in a tense voice, "I can't see the next flag. Can you?" Visibility had dropped to zero. Ahead and behind, to the right and to the left, there was nothing but white. It was like being inside a giant Ping-Pong ball.

The two women sat for a moment and talked about what to do. They decided on a plan. Jenn strapped on her goggles, pulled her hood down around her face, and opened the door. The wind nearly tore it out of her grasp. She climbed down onto the ice and made her way around to the front of the Spryte. Tania crawled into the driver's seat and waited.

Flags and familiar landmarks quickly disappear in the blowing snow of a whiteout.

Jenn began slowly walking forward, bending into the wind, straining to see through the driving snow. After taking a dozen steps, she stopped and turned around to make sure she could still see the Spryte. It was starting to fade in the blowing snow. If she lost sight of it, she would be in trouble. She took a few more steps, then stopped. A spot of red had appeared in the white nothingness ahead. It was the next flag.

Jenn waved her arms, and Tania drove up to meet her. Together they moved up beside the flag and stopped. Once again Jenn walked ahead until she could just see the next flag in line, and again Tania followed in the Spryte. After they reached the fourth flag, Jenn climbed back up inside the vehicle to warm up. It was Tania's turn next.

Quite unexpectedly, the wind died down enough so that first one flag, then another, appeared out of the whiteness in front of them. "Hey, I can see two!" cried Tania. Two flags were all they needed. Jenn shouted "Floor it!" Tania tromped on the gas pedal, and the Spryte lurched forward. When they reached the first flag, they could still see two more ahead. It was enough to keep going. Thirty minutes later the two women heaved sighs of relief as the Spryte rumbled into camp. Their home on the sea ice had never looked so good.

At the crater rim on Mount Erebus, Antarctica's most active volcano

3

Fire and Ice

"Good morning, good morning! It's a beautiful day in Mc-Murdo, and the helos are all up and flying!" Robin Abbott's cheery greeting went floating out over the airways. It was eight o'clock, and she had just begun morning "comms," her daily radio communication with groups of scientists working at field camps far from the station.

At remote sites within a two-hundred-mile radius of Mc-Murdo, researchers in tents and huts crouched by their radios and listened intently to Robin's lively voice. She was their link to McMurdo—their primary connection to the lifeline of support and supplies that they needed to survive in the wilds of Antarctica.

Perched on the edge of her chair in the cramped Helo Ops office, with notes in one hand and microphone in the other, Robin continued: "We've currently got sunshine and ten-knot winds. But Mac Center says the satellite maps show we could be in for a big change as the day progresses, so be aware of that."

As helicopter operations coordinator in McMurdo, Robin coordinated helicopter flights with the needs of scientists throughout the summer research season. Weather permitting, six helicopters flew dozens of missions a day, six days a week—shuttling people from place to place and delivering equipment, food, fuel, and other supplies to distant field camps. It was

41

Robin Abbott
directs helicopter
traffic from her
office in McMurdo.

Robin's job to figure out which helicopters would carry out
what tasks each day and then juggle the pieces of a complex
schedule that was always at the mercy of the fickle weather. It
was a hectic, stressful job with a lot of responsibility.

After giving the weather update and a brief report of what
was going on around the station, Robin contacted the field
camps individually. She worked her way down the list of science
teams, asking each group about the weather conditions where
they were, finding out what supplies they needed, and letting
them know if they were scheduled for a helicopter visit that day.
Everyone understood, however, that the schedule was always
subject to change.

"Sierra-Zero-Eight-One, how do you copy?" Robin's voice
came crackling over the radio that was set up in one corner of

the hut. Demetria Newsome listened as Phil Kyle, the scientist in charge of S-081, chatted with Robin and told her what the weather was like at their camp, eleven thousand feet above McMurdo on the steep slopes of Mount Erebus.

Rising up from the center of Ross Island, Mount Erebus towers above the surrounding polar landscape. It is a majestic mountain, cloaked in shining ice. Beneath that ice lies fire. Mount Erebus is Antarctica's tallest and most active volcano.

A plume of steam escapes from the Erebus crater.

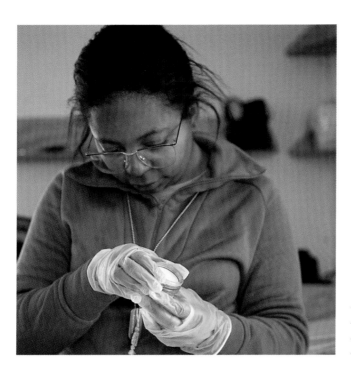

Demetria Newsome removes a filter from an air sampling device.

Demetria looked up from her work and glanced out one of the hut's windows. It was beautiful outside—unusually clear and calm. The helicopter that was supposed to arrive at mid-morning shouldn't have any problems landing. It was so clear that she could see mountains and glaciers hundreds of miles away in the interior of the continent. On days like this, living on Erebus felt like being suspended in the air, high above the rest of the world.

Through another window, Demetria looked up at the mountaintop that loomed above them at 12,500 feet. The volcano's summit was shrouded in clouds and its own steamy plume. "We won't see much of the crater today," she remarked to one of

Phil's Ph.D. students, Ed Klimasauskas. The two of them were carefully removing discs of filter paper from small air filters and sealing the discs in plastic bags.

"By the looks of that plume, I doubt we'll see much of anything!" Ed exclaimed. "But we'll soon find out. Just two more filters to go, and we can head on up to collect the next set of samples."

As she stripped off her plastic lab gloves, Demetria realized that if she were back home in Baltimore, Maryland, she'd just be starting her tenth-grade chemistry class at Paul Laurence Dunbar Community High School. Demetria was a high school teacher, one of the first ever to travel to Antarctica with the U.S. Antarctic Program and experience firsthand what it is like to do research on the continent. For the last week, Demetria had been helping the scientists of S-081 sample the gases that rise from the volcano's huge crater. What would her students think if they could see her here?

Twenty minutes later, she and Ed were outside in the cold, dry air, stowing their backpacks on a snowmobile. Ed offered to drive. Demetria climbed on behind him, and moments later they were whizzing along an icy trail that led up the mountainside toward the crater. The trail wound around great masses of jet black volcanic rock and twisting towers of ice. From the top of each tower, steamy vapor puffed like smoke from a chimney. The ice towers formed over cracks and holes in the ground that led up from the interior of the volcano.

Farther on, the trail became very steep. "Hang on!" Ed called out as the snowmobile tilted at a crazy angle. Demetria hung on but was ready to jump if they tipped too far. After a few more scary twists and turns, the trail ended abruptly about five hundred feet below the crater rim. Ed brought the snow-mobile to a screeching halt, and Demetria hopped off, glad the ride was over. They would go the rest of the way on foot.

As they started the climb up to the crater rim, Demetria looked back down the mountainside toward camp. She could barely see it—they were moving up into the clouds and steam that hung over the crater. The air around them was wet and warm and tinged with the sharp smell of sulfur. At this altitude, the air was also very thin—it contained less oxygen. She and Ed walked slowly, stopping every few minutes to catch their breath.

Steamy vapor puffs from an ice tower on the slopes of Mount Erebus.

Demetria checks the air sampling equipment near the crater rim.

They moved across a weird unearthly landscape. Scattered on the hillside were lava "bombs," rounded masses of lava that had been blown out of the crater during eruptions. The ground was littered with black volcanic crystals, each one to two inches long and about a half inch wide. With each step, the crystals underfoot clinked together with a soft musical sound.

Higher and higher they climbed. It was getting warmer, and the fog was thicker. The rotten-egg smell of sulfur was chokingly strong. Demetria stopped to pick up a crystal that had caught her eye. When she looked up, Ed was gone, lost in mist up ahead. "Hey, wait for me," she called, hurrying to catch up. She was out of breath by the time she rejoined him. Huffing and puffing, they struggled up the last few yards, and suddenly they were standing on the crater rim.

If it had been clear, they would have been able to see all the way across Erebus's enormous yawning crater and look down on the lava lake far below at its center. But Ed had been right. The volcano's thick plume completely blotted out any view. Demetria couldn't see more than a few feet in any direction.

Demetria went over to check the air sampling equipment that was set up just back from the crater's edge. "Okay, everything looks good," she called out, "Start it up!" Ed started a portable generator that powered several small pumps, each connected to an air filter. The pumps made a soft pucka-pucka-pucka sound as they drew in the smelly air rising up from the volcano and pumped it through the filters.

While the pumps worked, the two researchers crawled over to the rim of the crater and peered down. They couldn't see anything but white mist. But they could hear distant rumblings and an occasional hiss of steam. Erebus is a very active volcano and working at the crater's edge was a bit scary.

After twenty minutes, Ed shut off the generator, and he and Demetria carefully detached the filters from the pumps. Trapped on the thin paper discs inside each filter were traces of the chemicals that Erebus constantly spews into the air. The scientists of S-081 wanted to find out how much sulfur, chlorine, and other substances the volcano released into the Antarctic environment every day. When Ed and Demetria got back to the hut, they would remove the paper discs from these filters and get them ready to ship back to the United States for analysis.

As Ed and Demetria headed back down the steep crystal-covered slope, they heard the sound of an unseen helicopter in the distance. They hurried down to the snowmobile—maybe they could get back to camp before it took off again.

Back in McMurdo, Robin Abbott glanced up at the clock in her office. Ten o'clock, and things were still pretty much on schedule. The crew of *Gentle 11* had just called in to report they had landed at the Erebus hut. After they returned to McMurdo and refueled, they were scheduled to stop at Cape Bird, a field camp run by the New Zealand Antarctic Program at the northern end of Ross Island. *Gentle 14* and *Gentle 10* had radioed to say that there were low clouds settling into some of the valleys in the mountains across McMurdo Sound.

Just then the radio crackled, and the wavering voice of a pilot in an airborne helicopter filled the room: "This is *Gentle One-Six.* Cape Crozier is socked in with dense cloud cover. We cannot land to deliver our load to S-156. Returning to McMurdo. Over."

"Here we go," Robin murmured to herself. The juggling act was about to begin.

———————— ⅄ ————————

Fiona Hunter stood in front of the windows of the hut at Cape Bird and looked out at the icebergs in the sound while she finished her cup of tea. When she had checked in with Scott Base early that morning, the radio operator there had told her that Robin Abbott had arranged for one of the American helicopters to come out to Cape Bird around noon to drop off some supplies they needed. Scott Base—McMurdo's nearest neighbor—is the New Zealand Antarctic Program's main research station on Ross Island. The two stations often work together to provide helicopters for scientists.

It was time for Fiona to get out and visit her own neighbors before the helicopter arrived. Marj Wright, her research assistant, was still asleep. With twenty-four hours of daylight every

*Fiona Hunter,
surrounded by
Adélie penguins at
Cape Bird*

day, they tended to keep strange hours. Fiona grabbed her parka
and a pair of binoculars and set out along the narrow path that
led down from the hut to the rookery where sixty thousand
Adélie penguins had taken up residence for the season.

Fiona had spent the last ten years of her life studying seabirds
in cold remote places—the Shetland Islands, Greenland, the
Aleutian Islands, Antarctica. This was her second season at
Cape Bird, where she was studying mating behavior and repro-
duction in Adélies. She stopped on the path for a moment and
looked around. Except for the hut, there were no signs of civi-
lization in any direction. She loved being able to live and work
in wild unspoiled places like this.

But there were drawbacks to working in this frozen frontier.
A few weeks earlier, Fiona had gone snowblind. She'd left her
sunglasses off for just an hour, but that was enough time for
the sunlight reflecting off snow and ice to damage her eyes.
Eight hours later they had streamed with tears and burned as if

they had sand in them. For several days, she'd had to avoid the light and keep her eyes covered while they gradually healed.

Fiona rounded a ridge and looked up at the thousands of black-and-white birds that covered the hillsides. Adélie penguins had been nesting at Cape Bird for at least seven hundred years. Every October they returned to the rookery and wasted no time getting on with courtship, mating, and egg laying.

For years, scientists had thought that Adélie penguins were monogamous, that is, each bird had only one partner during the breeding season. But more recent research showed that many Adélies mate with several partners each spring. That raised some questions: When a female penguin mates with several different males, which one is the father of her chicks? Do some male penguins end up feeding and caring for chicks that are not theirs? Fiona was trying to answer those questions at Cape Bird.

Two Adélie penguins display to each other during courtship.

Picking her way carefully through the rookery, Fiona quietly approached her study site, where a group of about ninety penguins nested on a small rise of land. She had chosen this site the previous year and, with the help of several other scientists, had banded the birds and taken blood samples from them. The blood had been analyzed to establish a record of the genetic material unique to each individual. Fiona had ended up with a DNA "fingerprint" for every penguin at the site.

At the start of this season, as the penguins returned to the rookery to breed, Fiona and Marj had carefully watched the banded penguins at the study site, noting who mated with whom. It was exhausting work because the birds were active around the clock. When the female penguins had finally settled down and laid their eggs, the month-long wait for hatching had begun.

Through her binoculars, Fiona scanned the penguins at the study site as they sat on their stony nests. As one penguin stood up to stretch, Fiona spotted a tiny hole in its egg. It was hatching! Fiona held her breath and listened intently. All around her, above the loud calls of adult penguins, she could hear the faint high-pitched chirps of tiny Adélie chicks. Eggs were hatching everywhere!

Fiona smiled and slipped her binoculars back inside her parka. She'd have to go and wake Marj. The wait was over. As the chicks in the study site hatched, the two women would weigh and measure each one and take a tiny sample of its blood. That would keep them busy for several weeks.

Months later, when the blood samples were analyzed, Fiona would learn the genetic makeup of each chick. Then she would be able to match up the DNA fingerprints of parents and offspring. By comparing that information with her data on

*Fiona picks up a
newly hatched
Adélie chick* (above)
*and cradles it in her
hands* (right).

An Adélie chick is warmed by its parent.

mating, she would be able to figure out which male penguins had fathered which chicks. Knowing that would help answer many questions about penguin parentage.

As Fiona hurried back to the hut, she noticed that low gray clouds were closing in around the cape, rapidly blotting out the view of the icebergs offshore and the glaciers above the rookery. She'd give Scott Base a call and tell them to notify Robin Abbott about the sudden change in the weather. There would be no helicopters landing at Cape Bird today. But that was all right. The chicks were hatching, and there was so much to do.

———— ⊁⊁ ————

Robin hung up the phone after talking with Scott Base—Cape Bird was off the schedule. Three other field camps radioed in to tell her that they were socked in with clouds too. The weather was deteriorating all around Ross Island and in the mountains across the sound. The helicopter schedule was changing minute by minute as pilots scrambled to fly where the weather hadn't yet made it impossible.

A meteorologist from the weather center popped his head in the door: "Robin, we've just gone to Condition 2." McMurdo's weather was rated as Condition 3, 2, or 1, with Condition 3 being the best. The helicopters were grounded when the rating went to Condition 2. Those out flying would try to return to the station to wait for the weather to improve.

Robin grabbed the radio and began contacting the field camps that were still expecting a helicopter that day. She'd tell them maybe tomorrow or the next day . . . weather permitting.

———— ⊁⊁ ————

A hundred and fifty miles away, on a windswept glacier in the Allan Hills, Nelia Dunbar bent close to the radio, straining to hear Robin's voice above the crackle of static. The radio sat on one end of a long table that ran the length of the Weather-Port, the heated shelter that served as the camp's kitchen, laboratory, and office space. At the other end of the table, Bill McIntosh and Rich Esser were busy making lunch.

There was a pause, and Nelia spoke loudly into the radio microphone: "Robin, this is Sierra-One-Eight-Two. You are broken and faint. Please repeat. Over." There was more static, but this time Nelia caught the reply. She acknowledged the message, signed off, and turned to Bill and Rich. "Change of plan. The helos are all grounded due to weather in McMurdo. We won't be getting our flight today."

"Well, we could collect samples on one of the Hairpins," Bill suggested.

Nelia peeled back the square of fabric that served as a window in the WeatherPort and looked out. Beyond the camp, a seemingly endless expanse of blue-white ice stretched to the horizon, interrupted here and there in the distance by the faint silhouettes of mountaintops all but buried beneath thousands of feet of ice. The only thing that seemed alive was the wind as it screamed past the camp, relentlessly driving snow across the frozen landscape. "Well, the weather's not bad," Nelia mused.

Volcanologist Nelia Dunbar, in the Allan Hills

"Let's go sample at Hairpin 1. There'll be time to process the samples when we get back."

Nelia Dunbar was a volcanologist—a scientist who studies volcanoes—from the New Mexico Institute of Technology. After nearly ten seasons in Antarctica, Nelia had seen much of the continent and its volcanoes.

The glaciers in the Allan Hills contain deposits of volcanic ash, traces of ancient volcanic eruptions. These ash deposits occur as narrow bands that run like faint gray ribbons through

Drifts form quickly as snow blows through the Allan Hills camp.

the ice. Nelia, Bill, and Rich had come to this wild windy place to collect samples of the ancient volcanic ash.

After lunch the three researchers pulled on windproof jackets and pants and strapped sturdy crampons onto their boots. The sharp metal cleats of the crampons made it possible to walk on ice. "What did we ever do without handwarmers?" Nelia asked as she slipped two of the little heat-generating packets into the ends of her mittens. Rich shoved the door open, and they stepped out into the wind.

Snow had drifted around everything—the two tents they used for sleeping, their snowmobiles, and all their boxes of supplies. Drifts formed with amazing speed around any obstacle in the wind's path. "We're going to have to dig out the food boxes when we get back," Bill said as they walked past the row of supplies, "or they'll be completely buried by tomorrow."

After clearing the drifts from around the snowmobiles, the scientists strapped a chainsaw onto the back of one, loaded a big ice chest onto another, and piled survival gear onto a third. It took a few minutes to get the cold machines started. At last they were off, rumbling across the ice with the wind at their backs.

Bill led the way across the glacier toward the ash band called Hairpin 1. It looked like a two-foot-wide shadow in the ice, a smoky gray streak that went on and on, curving this way and that. They followed it for several miles before Bill pulled up sharply and stopped.

As far as they could see, there was nothing but ice—barren and dazzlingly bright. Blowing snow twisted and surged and streamed across its surface. Bracing himself against the wind, Bill started up the chainsaw. As the blade sliced easily into the glacier, he began carving out slabs of ice from the ash band. Nelia piled the slabs into the ice chest. It took about twenty

The wind-polished surface of a blue ice glacier stretches toward the horizon.

Nelia (left) jots down notes as Bill McIntosh cuts samples from an ash band that runs through the glacier.

minutes to get what they needed. Then they chipped a hole in the ice and drove in a flag-topped bamboo pole to mark the site.

On the trip back, the scientists had to drive into the wind. They hunched down behind the windshields of the snowmobiles, but there was no escape. By the time they got back to camp, their noses, cheeks, and fingers were numb from the cold.

After warming up by shoveling the snowdrifts away from their supplies and drinking hot orange drink, Nelia and Bill started to extract the volcanic ash from the ice they'd brought back. They set up several camp stoves, stuffed the chunks of ice into large pots, and set them on the stoves to melt.

An hour later, when the ice had melted, the scientists carefully filtered the water to collect all the volcanic ash it contained. They ended up with a small amount of what looked like fine gray dust.

Bill put a bit of the ash on a slide and looked at it under a microscope. When light struck the slide at a certain angle, the ash was transformed from drab dust into a sparkling collection of colorful particles.

Volcanic ash is made up of tiny shards of volcanic glass. Using a variety of techniques, scientists can analyze the microscopic bits of glass in an ash sample and figure out what minerals they contain. Every volcano produces ash that has a unique mineral content, like a fingerprint. And just as fingerprints can be matched to specific people, scientists can match ash deposits to the volcano that produced them.

Many of the world's volcanoes have been fingerprinted by volcanologists. By comparing the fingerprints of volcanic ash bands in Antarctica with those of the world's volcanoes, Nelia hoped to pinpoint which volcanoes produced the ash that is trapped in the glaciers of the Allan Hills.

The scientists of S-182 also hoped that their ash samples would help answer a fundamental question about glaciers in Antarctica: How old are they? Ice itself can't be dated. But back in their laboratories in the United States, the scientists would be able to date the ash samples using a technique called radiometric dating. Once the scientists knew how old an ash sample was, they would also know how old the ice was around it.

What was the climate like in Antarctica ten thousand, one hundred thousand, or a million years ago? When scientists figure out how old the glaciers are that cover the Antarctic landscape, they will be closer to answering those questions.

Beyond the gleaming base of the Canada Glacier lies ice-covered Lake Hoare.

4

Life at Lake Hoare

Rae Spain sat perched on the roof of the main hut, where she had just finished fastening down an antennae cable that was connected to the radio equipment inside the building. She gave the cable a final tug to make sure it would stay put in the 120-mile-an-hour winds that sometimes roared through Taylor Valley. Satisfied it was secure, she stretched out her legs and took a moment to enjoy the view.

The main hut was the largest building in the Lake Hoare field camp. Together with a few smaller huts and a sprinkling of yellow mountain tents, it stood on the gravelly shore of ice-covered Lake Hoare at the base of the massive Canada Glacier. In the early morning light, the glacier looked like polished white marble.

The Canada Glacier is one of many glaciers that spill down from the mountains around Taylor Valley in the barren region known as the McMurdo Dry Valleys. One of the coldest driest deserts in the world, the Dry Valleys are a strange mixture of glaciers, rocky slopes, and lakes that are permanently covered with ice.

"Hey, Rae!" came a voice from the ground, "when you're finished up there, could you give me a hand setting up these solar panels?"

Rae grabbed her tool bag. "Sure, Steve!" she shouted and made her way over to the edge of the roof to climb down.

Rae Spain was a carpenter with thirteen seasons of experience working in Antarctica. She had built everything from huts, walkways, and laboratories to special equipment for scientists, such as solar-heated boxes for sensitive instruments and a device for collecting snowflakes thirty feet above the ground. For years she had worked in subzero temperatures, battled hurricane-force winds, and endured raging blizzards.

Rae Spain assembles a portable hut on Lake Hoare.

Rae and Steve Mulholland, also a carpenter, were at Lake Hoare to put the final touches on the camp. The main hut and some of the smaller structures were not quite finished, even though scientists were already living and working there.

Just beyond the main hut, Steve was unpacking large solar panels that would provide the Lake Hoare camp with much of the electricity needed to run computers and other pieces of equipment—including some of the appliances in the hut's kitchen.

"Good site for solar panels," Rae said, squinting at the sun overhead. "It's a lot sunnier here in the Valleys than some other places I've been." Rae remembered the season she had spent at tiny Siple Station in West Antarctica, hundreds of miles from McMurdo. Siple was famous for its horrendous weather. Ten feet of snow fell at the station each year, and blizzards sometimes lasted for weeks at a time. Rae and the other construction workers at Siple frequently had to work outside. More often than not, they could hardly see what they were building because of the blowing snow. The main part of the station was literally buried under forty feet of snow—people had to climb down ladders to get into the buildings.

After bolting together the first set of solar panels, Rae stopped to slip off her heavy jacket. The air temperature was just a few degrees above zero, but Rae was used to much colder places. During three seasons at the South Pole station, she had often worked outside in temperatures around sixty degrees below zero, with a windchill of more than a hundred degrees below zero. It was so cold at the South Pole that the grease in her power tools sometimes froze while she was using them. And it was always too cold to use real concrete in construction. For building foundations, the construction crew used what they jokingly called "Antarctic concrete"—just plain water. In minutes, water froze into ice that was as hard and permanent as real concrete.

After the solar panels were up, Rae headed inside the main hut. Her next job was to install some cabinets in the kitchen. She kicked the loose gravel from her boots and heaved open the hut's heavy air-lock door. It was warm and snug and bright inside and, compared to many other Antarctic field camps, quite luxurious. The Lake Hoare hut had skylights, and in the kitchen there was a real stove, refrigerator, and microwave oven.

More than a dozen scientists were based at Lake Hoare. They were all involved in the Dry Valleys Long Term Ecological Research (LTER) project, an in-depth study of the Taylor Valley that would go on for many years. The LTER researchers were investigating everything from the soils on the valley floor to the windswept mountain peaks that towered above it. They were searching for answers to all sorts of questions: How much snow fell on the valley each year? What kinds of microbes lived in the ice-covered lakes, and how did they get the nutrients they needed to survive? How much meltwater did the glaciers add to the valley's lakes? The goal of the LTER project was to learn as much as possible about this cold polar desert and figure out how all of its different components—glaciers, lakes, weather, soils—interacted to create one of the most unusual ecosystems in the world.

With so many scientists working at the camp, the main hut was usually bustling with activity. But it was early, and there were only two people inside when Rae walked in. Gayle Dana and Karen Lewis were sitting side by side at the hut's long table, poring over several maps. They smiled a greeting to Rae and then went back to planning their day.

Karen Lewis (left) ***and Gayle Dana, atop a glacier in the Taylor Valley***

"Okay, if we go this way," said Gayle, tracing a line with her finger on a map of the glaciers around Lake Hoare, "we can avoid this crevassed area entirely."

Karen studied Gayle's suggested route across the upper part of the Howard Glacier—their destination that day. After thinking for a moment, she nodded. "It's a bit longer. But we won't have to do any backtracking that way. We can ask Bill what he thinks when he gets here too."

Gayle was from the Desert Research Institute at the University of Nevada, where she was working on a Ph.D. in hydrology—the study of how water moves through ecosystems. Karen was a graduate student at the Institute for Arctic and Alpine

Research at the University of Colorado, and glaciers were her area of special interest. The two women were studying the glaciers in the Taylor Valley as part of the LTER project. They were interested in how the glaciers changed from season to season and year to year: Were they growing larger or smaller? How much water did they gain each year as a result of snow accumulating on their surfaces? How much water did they lose through melting, and where did the water go?

Gayle sat back and looked at her watch. "The helo is supposed to arrive at about nine-fifteen. We should start getting ready."

They began piling equipment beside the table—coils of rope, bunches of ice screws and carabiners, a bundle of long bamboo poles, ice axes, and backpacks filled with water, food, and survival gear. Karen put fresh battery packs into their handheld radios, while Gayle tested the compact drill they would be using. They put on their mountaineering boots and climbing harnesses and carried everything out to the level spot above the hut where the helicopter would land.

Gayle stood looking thoughtfully at the drill bit that lay beside their drill. "You know, that bit is going to get dull pretty fast, cutting into glacier ice," she said. "I'm going to get on the radio to Mimi. Maybe she can find something to sharpen it with and send it out with Bill on the helo."

———————— \\ ————————

From the window of her office in the Berg Field Center, Mimi Fujino could see nearly all of McMurdo Station—except the helo pad. But she was pretty sure the helicopter bound for Lake Hoare hadn't departed yet. There might still be time to find the tools Gayle needed and get them on the flight. Mimi hurried through the old wooden building to one of several

Mimi Fujino examines her stock of tents at the Berg Field Center.

stockrooms that were filled from floor to ceiling with expedition gear and supplies.

Mimi was the supervisor of the Berg Field Center, or BFC as everyone called it. The BFC was McMurdo's supply hub for field expeditions and camps. It was packed with every imaginable item of camping, mountaineering, and polar survival gear.

It was Mimi's job to see that the sixty to seventy groups of scientists who traveled into the field every season were fitted out with the equipment they needed, from tents, sleds, and stoves to portable toilets. She made sure that scientists knew how to use the equipment they were issued and that they were trained to survive being stranded in a blizzard, travel safely across glaciers and sea ice, and give first aid to a person suffering from frostbite.

Mimi's search took her through a maze of shelves stocked with stoves, candles, pots and pans, axes, ropes, crampons, and tools. She found what she needed high on a shelf and then hurried downstairs. With luck she could catch Bill McCormick before he went down to the helo pad. Bill was one of several mountaineers who worked at the BFC as a survival school instructor and field guide. He was going to help Gayle and Karen cross the Howard Glacier that day. A few years earlier, Mimi had been a survival school instructor too. She had run the sea-ice school and taught scientists and support staff the survival skills they needed to travel and work safely on the sea ice.

Mimi caught up to Bill just as he was leaving. "Take these along, would you, Bill? Gayle needs them for the drill bits."

Bill stuffed the tools into his pack. "No problem," he said with a smile. He grabbed his ice ax, put on his sunglasses, and headed out the door.

Karen was the first to hear the faint drone of the distant helicopter. "They're coming!" she called to Gayle. The two women pulled on their jackets and gloves and ran up to the helo pad, where they crouched beside their gear. The sound of the helicopter got louder and louder. Then suddenly there it was, thundering up over the top of the Canada Glacier. It circled the camp once before coming in to land. Gayle and Karen covered their faces as the helicopter settled to earth and its whirling rotor sent sand and gravel flying in every direction.

They scrambled aboard, and soon the helicopter was airborne again. It soared across Lake Hoare and then climbed up, up, up to the top of the Howard Glacier on the other side of the valley. When the helicopter landed, Bill, Gayle, and Karen jumped out. Moments later they stood alone on the glacier, three small dark dots in a sea of white.

The glacier stretched to the jagged mountain peaks on either side and cascaded down toward the valley floor, where miles below, their camp was just a speck beside Lake Hoare. Karen scanned the white moonscape of ice, hundreds of feet thick, thousands of years old.

The sunlight reflecting off the ice was blindingly bright. Gayle squinted against the glare as she pulled out her map and

Gayle (left) *and Karen scale the glacier's slippery surface.*

turned to Bill, who was studying the glacier through his binoculars. "We want to put the first pole in somewhere around here," she said, showing him a spot on the map, "and then work our way down the glacier in a sort of zigzag pattern, putting in poles every so often as we go."

"Well, we definitely want to avoid that area," Bill said, pointing to a place off to the right where gaping crevasses split the ice. For several minutes, they talked over possible routes down the glacier. They settled on what looked like the safest one, and then they set out, single file.

The face of the glacier sloped down gently at first. The ice they walked on had been polished by the wind and was very slippery. Without crampons it would have been difficult to stand up. Gradually the icy terrain became steeper and steeper. The sound of steel biting into ice echoed through the air as the three climbers used their ice axes to chop out steps and handholds in the side of the glacier.

At the bottom of the steep slope, the ice leveled out. This was where Gayle wanted to put the first bamboo pole. She set to work drilling out a narrow hole in the hard glacial ice. When the hole was several feet deep, she stepped back and Karen drove one of the long poles down into it.

"We plan to put about ninety of these poles into this glacier," Karen explained to Bill as she and Gayle carefully measured the length of the bamboo pole sticking up above the surface of the ice. "We'll measure each pole when we put it in and then again at the end of the season. Over the next few years, all the poles we will have put into the Howard—and into two other glaciers in the valley—will be measured many times."

Gayle went on to explain how the measurements would show the glaciers' change over time: "If we come back next year and

Bill McCormick (left) **and Karen get ready to drill a hole in the glacier for one of the bamboo poles.**

find that more of each pole is sticking out of the ice, we'll know that the glacier has decreased in size. If the poles are 'shorter,' we'll know the glacier has grown. And from the measurements we've taken, we'll be able to calculate how much

*Karen drills into
the hard glacier ice.*

mass—water, actually—the glaciers are gaining or losing from
year to year."

While Karen recorded the measurements, Gayle took a picture
of the site and marked its exact location on her map. Then they
packed up the drill and resumed their trek down the glacier.

Every so often, they stopped to drill a hole and set another
pole into the ice. The surface was steep in many places, and the

*Gayle measures a
bamboo pole.*

climbing was hard. Several times they had to use ropes to rappel down sheer ice cliffs. By noon they were tired and hungry, and they stopped to devour sandwiches and trail mix and Cadbury bars.

Midafternoon arrived, and they were halfway down the glacier and still making good time. Then they ran into the snow.

Bill pulled out his binoculars and scanned the even surface of snow that covered the glacier ahead of them. It was impossible to tell how deep the snow was—or whether the ice beneath it was solid or riddled with crevasses. Drifting snow often forms bridges over cracks in the ice, creating a smooth surface that looks thick and solid but is too thin to support a person's weight. Stepping in the wrong place could mean plunging to certain death in a deep crevasse.

"There's no way around," Bill said, tightening the harness around his waist. "We'll have to cross it, so let's rope up."

Bill uncoiled a long rope and tied one end into his harness. Gayle tied on in the middle of the rope, and Karen tied on at the other end. When Bill was sure their knots and harnesses were all secure, he started out across the snow. Step by careful step he went, testing the snow in front of him by probing it with the handle of his ice ax. Gayle and Karen followed, also probing the snow and keeping the lengths of rope that separated them fairly taut. If one person broke through the snow and slipped into a crevasse, the rope would hold them while the other two pulled their fallen companion back to safety.

It was slow going, but they made steady progress. Then suddenly Bill's ice ax slid too easily into the snow. He could tell by the way it felt that there was no ice beneath the snow in front of him. He backed up and probed the snow to his left. It seemed firm. He moved in that direction a few dozen feet and then advanced slowly, probing the snow again and again. It was solid, and they moved on.

When they finally reached snow-free ice again, they undid the safety line that connected them and sat down to rest. After just a few minutes, Gayle glanced at her watch. "Sorry, guys," she said, "but we've got to keep moving. It's already three-thirty." They had several more miles to go—and many more poles to set into the ice—before they reached the spot near the bottom of the glacier where a helicopter would pick them up. Wearily they shouldered their packs, grabbed poles and drill and ropes, and continued down the ice.

It was nearly seven o'clock in the evening before the helicopter touched down at the Lake Hoare camp. Gayle and Karen jumped out and hurried away toward the hut. They waved good-bye to Bill and the crew as the aircraft passed overhead. Fatigue showed on their sunburned faces. It had been a long day, and the job wasn't finished. Tomorrow they would be going back up onto the Howard to put in the last dozen poles.

Two bowls of chili each helped restore their strength, at least enough for them to repack their climbing gear, make lunches, and finalize their plans for the following day. Then they trudged out to their small yellow tents on the gravelly lakeshore. Curled up in puffy down sleeping bags, they fell asleep beneath the shadow of the Canada Glacier.

The scientists' tents at Lake Hoare are dwarfed by the Canada Glacier.

Views of a Polar Desert

Cheryl Hallam sat at her computer in her office in McMurdo's Crary Lab. The image on the screen in front of her was bright and colorful. Beneath a vivid blue sky, there was a broad valley bordered on either side by chocolate-brown mountains and snow-white glaciers. It was unmistakably a scene from the Dry Valleys.

Cheryl clicked the mouse, and the image on the screen began to change. It looked as if she were flying down the valley, soaring past the mountains and glaciers. For several seconds, she kept on the same straight course. Then, with another click of the mouse, she veered off toward a mountain peak on the left side of the screen. The image of the mountain grew larger and larger, as if she were flying right up to it, so close that the different layers in the rock showed up as bands of light and dark. Another click and the mountain disappeared as Cheryl plotted a new course through the landscape on the screen.

Frost polygons decorate the barren slopes of a Dry Valley landscape.

79

Cheryl was a digital cartographer with the United States Geological Survey, and she was in Antarctica developing a new tool for scientists to use to explore the continent. Digital cartography involves using computers to make maps. By combining aerial photographs, contour drawings, satellite images, and using the latest in computer software, a digital cartographer can create very accurate and realistic three-dimensional maps. These maps can be projected onto a computer screen and experienced in a way that no two-dimensional map can be.

Cheryl ran through the program a few more times, looking for places where she could improve the image. In McMurdo, Cheryl spent most of her time in her office, showing scientists how digital cartography worked and letting them "fly" through the Dry Valley landscape on her computer screen. It was a great way for researchers to get a first impression of different parts of the valleys where they would be working. And it certainly was more fun than reading paper maps!

Cheryl Hallam checks a map in her office in the Crary Lab.

One of Cheryl's computer images of glaciers and mountains in the Dry Valleys

But Cheryl was the first to admit that a computer simulation was no substitute for a real-life view of the Dry Valleys or the chance to explore them.

———— ⑈ ————

Laura Powers watched the rugged mountains flash by and then pressed her face against the window of the helicopter and peered down. Five hundred feet below, the ground looked like a patchwork quilt made up of irregularly shaped patches of rocky soil. The patches were called frost polygons, and they formed as a result of the repeated freezing and thawing of the ground in this polar desert.

The landscape they were flying over could have been from some alien world on a far distant planet. It was drier than the Sahara and bitterly cold, and it looked empty and lifeless. But Laura knew that there was life down there. Chances were good that the ground below was teeming with tiny worms called nematodes.

There are many different kinds of nematodes. Some types are very common, particularly in soil. A handful of dirt from almost any place on earth probably contains at least a few nematodes.

The minute nematodes that live in the Dry Valleys were first discovered in the 1920s by early explorers. But it wasn't until seventy years later that scientists began studying these worms that live on a continent where few other organisms can survive. Laura was a soil ecologist from Colorado State University. For the last few years, Antarctic nematodes had been the focus of her research.

Laura caught sight of a rocky plateau further down the valley—just the kind of site she was looking for. She pressed the button on her ICS and spoke into the tiny microphone attached to her helmet: "Geoff, do you see that plateau on the left, about halfway up the side of the valley? That's where I'd like to land."

The pilot spotted the site. "Got it," he answered. He changed course and brought the helicopter around for a closer look. Laura checked her watch. It would take about six hours to collect the soil samples they needed.

In the Dry Valleys, nematodes are at the top of a very simple food chain in the soil—other than the algae and bacteria that they eat, there are few other organisms in their environment. So it is relatively easy for scientists to study how nematodes respond to changes in their environment, how they help cycle nutrients in the soil, and how they survive the extremely cold, dry conditions that exist in this Antarctic desert.

As the helicopter touched down, Laura slid back the door and jumped out. She and the members of her research team—Melody Brown, Lisa Marlies, and John Freckman—quickly unloaded their things. Moments later the helicopter was gone.

Laura Powers (left) *and Melody Brown discuss a soil sample they hope will contain nematodes.*

Laura made a quick tour of the area, walking only in the narrow furrows in the ground that ran like natural pathways among the frost polygons. She chose eight polygons as the sites where they would collect soil samples. They paired up into two teams and got down to work.

Laura and Melody followed a furrow over to their first polygon. Stepping from rock to rock so as not to contaminate the soil with their boots, they walked out to the middle and knelt down on the cold ground. Melody took out several plastic bags and a small scoop from her backpack. With the scoop, Laura began to dig a small hole in the ground, scraping up the dry soil and pouring it into the plastic bag that Melody held open for her.

It was hard to believe that anything could live in soil so dry. But nematodes have a remarkable survival strategy. When their environment gets too dry, the tiny worms curl up and go into a state known as cryptobiosis. Cryptobiosis is a sort of suspended animation—the worms' normal life processes essentially stop. Nematodes can survive in this cryptobiotic state for years. When a bit of moisture is added to their environment again— perhaps a light dusting of snow on the ground with enough sunshine to melt it—the worms quickly return to normal.

When the first bag was full, Melody sealed it shut, labeled it, and stuffed it into an empty backpack. She held out another bag as Laura kept digging.

Laura wouldn't know what kinds of nematodes, or how many, were in the soil she was collecting until the samples had been processed. Back in their lab in McMurdo, her team would

In the lab at McMurdo, John Freckman and Lisa Marlies watch as Laura (center) carries out the next step in extracting nematodes from soil samples they collected.

wash and strain the gritty soil again and again to extract any microscopic worms it might contain.

Nematodes weren't uniformly distributed in the Dry Valleys. In some places, one scoop of soil contained hundreds of them. At other sites, the tiny worms were scarce. Why was this so? Were there more nutrients in some soils than in others? Did certain types of nematodes do better in different places or at different altitudes? Did they migrate through the soil? These were all questions Laura and her research team were trying to answer.

Melody sealed up the last bag of soil and stuffed it into the backpack, which was bulging with samples. She and Laura carried it between them as they picked their way back on the rocks to the furrowed path. They unloaded the samples into one of the ice chests they had brought along and then got ready to start on their next site.

Laura glanced over to where John and Lisa were working. They were still digging in their first polygon. Laura shivered and blew on her fingers to warm them. After kneeling on the ground for an hour, the cold had managed to seep through her many layers of clothing. By the time the helicopter came back to pick them up, she guessed they would all be pretty cold.

———————

Miles away, across two mountain ranges from where Laura and her team were working, Bonnie Bratina zipped open her tent and squinted out at Lake Vanda. It glittered like a blue-green jewel on the floor of Wright Valley.

Bonnie crawled out of her small mountain tent and stood for a moment in the faintly warm sunshine. It was absolutely still. Not a breath of wind stirred in this great wide valley where she and the three other members of S-041 had lived for the last three weeks. Their camp was on a tiny island near one end of ice-covered Lake Vanda.

The silence was broken by the clatter of pots and pans coming from the camp's big pyramid-shaped Scott tent where they did their cooking. Brad must be making breakfast. Bonnie glanced at her watch and discovered it was almost noon. They had worked very late last night.

Bonnie stepped inside the big tent. "That smells good," she said to the man hunched over the camp stove. Brad Stevenson, her research assistant, looked up from stirring something in a pan. "Well, I'm making fried potatoes—dehydrated, of course—and an omelet. Made with powdered eggs. But the coffee's real," he added with a laugh.

Lake Vanda sparkles in the sun.

Bonnie Bratina (right) and Brad Stevenson stride across Vanda's frozen surface on their way to the sampling site.

The smell of food soon attracted the other camp members—Bill Green and his assistant, Brian Stage. The four of them sat on the cots in the tent and ate omelets and laid plans for another day's work out on the lake. Bill and Brian were investigating Lake Vanda's unique water chemistry. Bonnie and Brad were both microbiologists who were studying the bacteria that lived beneath the ice.

After breakfast, the scientists walked down to the edge of their tiny island where two sleds lay on the rocky shore. They piled a day's supply of food and water into the sleds, strapped crampons onto their boots, and set out for their sampling site that lay two miles away across the ice.

Stepping onto the frozen surface of Lake Vanda is like entering a magic kingdom. The thick ice is extraordinarily clear.

A close-up of the ice on Lake Vanda

It is tinted delicate shades of blue and green and turquoise and filled with hairline cracks and silvery bubbles. The surface of the ice has been polished smooth by the wind, and when the sun is shining, the lake sparkles like a field of diamonds.

It took half an hour to reach the two Scott tents that were staked out on the ice near the center of the lake. Each tent covered a hole that had been drilled into the ice. Bill and Brian disappeared into one tent to do their work, and Bonnie and Brad crawled into the other.

In Bonnie's tent, the hole in the ice was close to the entrance, just off to one side. The hole—ten inches in diameter—looked like a giant eye, with a pale blue iris of ice crystals surrounding a pupil of blue-black water. Through this hole, Bonnie and Brad could reach the lake water far beneath the ice.

Each day they pumped water up from various depths and filtered out the bacteria it contained.

A huge coil of plastic tubing lay next to the hole. Lake Vanda was over two hundred feet deep, and they needed to filter samples of water from just under the ice all the way down to the lake bottom. Bonnie fed one end of the tubing into the hole and let it down slowly. Today they were going to filter bacteria out of the water at thirty, forty, and fifty meters below the ice.

Bonnie works at the sampling site on Lake Vanda.

Brad was counting the meter marks on the tubing as it disappeared down the hole. "Okay, that's thirty," he said. He helped Bonnie lash the tubing in place, and then he checked the pump. They used a small electric pump to bring the water up through the tube and send it through a filter.

"Look at this," Brad said, holding up the pump. "It's frozen up. We must have left a little water in it last night. How are we going to melt that ice inside?"

Bonnie thought for a moment. "Handwarmers!" she exclaimed. She dug two handwarmers out of her survival bag, unwrapped them, and shook them to start them heating. Brad taped them onto the pump with duct tape. They waited a few minutes, and sure enough, the ice in the pump began to melt.

"Okay, I'll fire up the generator," said Brad as he crawled out of the tent. "Turn on the pump when I get it going."

The generator stood out on the ice away from the tents. Brad yanked the starter cord, and after a bit of sputtering and stalling, the generator chugged to life. Bonnie turned on the pump, and with a whispery sucking sound, it began to draw water up the hose and pump it through the filter.

Two hours later, Bonnie shut off the pump and opened the filter. Inside was a circle of thin filter paper. Any bacteria in the water they had pumped up from thirty meters down were trapped on this thin sheet. With a tweezers, she carefully lifted out the paper and slipped it into a plastic ziplock bag. Brad put new paper in the filter, lowered the tubing down to forty meters, and started up the pump again.

It was eleven-thirty at night before they finally finished the day's sampling. Bill and Brian had left earlier, having finished their work more quickly. Bonnie and Brad pulled the tubing up out of the hole and drained the water out of it so that the tubing wouldn't freeze. The wind had come up and was tugging at the tent flaps. They were tired and wet and chilled to the bone as they began the long walk back to camp. But they were satisfied with their day's work on the frozen lake.

When they eventually finished collecting their bacteria samples at Lake Vanda, they would take the samples back to McMurdo. There they would cultivate the bacteria in laboratory dishes and run experiments on them. These experiments would help the scientists determine what kinds of nutrients the bacteria needed to live and grow and how they differed from bacteria in other lakes of the world.

The late-night sun had passed behind the mountains on the west side of Wright Valley. Most of Lake Vanda lay in a cold blue shadow. As the ice on the lake contracted in the cold, it gave off sharp cracking sounds—like whipcracks and rifle shots—that traveled from one end of the lake to the other and echoed through the valley. For the two young scientists heading back to camp, it was as if the lake beneath their feet had come to life.

At the very bottom of the world, a dome covers the main buildings of the Amundsen-Scott South Pole Station.

Farthest South

Wearing a T-shirt and ragged jeans, Julia Uberuaga sat in the heated cab of her D7 Caterpillar bulldozer. Her strong callused hands rested lightly on the hydraulic controls as sixty-two thousand pounds of mechanical power rumbled forward toward a snowdrift that was as high as the bulldozer. With a delicate touch, she manipulated the levers controlling the sixteen-foot steel blade. The blade tilted down and dug into the drift, slicing out a several-ton chunk of snow. She drove on, pushing the snow beyond the drift to where the landscape leveled out. She dumped the load of snow there and went back for more. Back and forth the bulldozer went, as the woman behind the controls reshaped the all-white landscape around Willy Field.

Julia—or Jules, as she was known to almost everyone—was a heavy equipment operator and a veteran of fifteen consecutive seasons in Antarctica. She had spent most of them moving snow at Willy Field, where ski-equipped airplanes land on runways made of snow.

It was a never-ending battle to keep the runways clear of drifts. Willy Field was about ten miles from McMurdo Station, out on the flat windy plain of the Ross Ice Shelf. Day after day, blowing snow swept across this frozen wasteland. The drifting snow constantly threatened to bury the buildings at Willy, as well as the runways. It was Jules's job to keep them clear.

93

Jules stopped the bulldozer and took a moment to survey her work. The huge drift was gone, transformed into a smooth, level surface. But she could see that the wind was already teasing the powdery snow into the air once again. It wouldn't be long before the drift would re-form. Jules didn't really mind. She loved moving snow and controlling the enormously powerful pieces of equipment she drove around all day.

Off in the distance, a plane started to taxi down the runway,

Jules Uberuaga and her bulldozer, at Willy Field

Scientists with the U.S. Antarctic Program arrive at the South Pole.

freshly groomed by the Willy Field crew. It was an LC-130 Hercules cargo plane. Jules sat back in her seat and watched the plane's propellers kick up a cloud of snow as it skimmed along on enormous skis. Airborne at last, it climbed slowly into the pale blue sky and headed south to the bottom of the world.

Qin Sun sat in the galley at the Amundsen-Scott South Pole Station and finished the last of her lunch. She had been at the

Qin Sun, with one of the light detectors used to study neutrinos

station for three weeks, and although the meals were good, she was getting hungry for some real Chinese food. A native of Shanghai, Qin (pronounced "Chin") was a Ph.D. student at Stockholm University in Sweden, where she was working on a degree in particle physics. Particle physicists study subatomic particles like protons, neutrons, and electrons.

Qin was especially interested in small, high-energy particles called neutrinos. Scientists think neutrinos come from black holes, quasars, and supernovas far beyond our galaxy. These mysterious particles are very difficult to study. But the possibility of investigating neutrinos in a new way had brought Qin from Sweden to the South Pole.

Finished with her lunch, Qin was anxious to get back to work. She checked the monitor on the galley wall. The weather report that scrolled continuously across the tiny screen said it was −40° F outside, but with very little wind. Qin zipped up her parka and put on her neck gaiter, hat, sunglasses, and mittens. She was ready to face the cold.

As she stepped outside, Qin's breath billowed out like a cloud in front of her face. She left the aluminum dome that covered the galley and the other main buildings and entered a long metal archway that led, like a tunnel, from the dome to the bright-white world outside. It was so intensely cold that there was no moisture in the air at all. The snow beneath her feet was powder dry. It squeaked like Styrofoam with every step she took.

Qin walked out into the sunshine—weak polar sunshine that was bright but not warm. By this time, Qin had gotten used to the stark South Pole landscape. It was empty and flat, without even a hill to break the monotony. Except for the dome and the few other structures scattered around the station, there was nothing but snow all the way to the horizon in every direction.

Qin crossed the skiway, where the planes from McMurdo landed and took off. Despite the cold, she did not hurry. The South Pole station sits atop nearly 9,500 feet of solid ice. Living here was like living on a mountain, and the high altitude left Qin gasping for breath if she moved too fast.

Her destination was a bright blue building a half mile from the dome. The "blue lab" was elevated above the ground so that blowing snow wouldn't bury it in drifts. Qin spent most of her time there, working with an international team of scientists who were constructing the largest neutrino detector in the world. And they were using the vastly thick ice sheet beneath the South Pole station to do it.

Neutrinos are elusive particles. They are so small and powerful that most of the time they pass right through the earth, undetected. But sometimes, neutrinos collide with atoms. When that happens, a tiny flash of blue light is given off. So while scientists cannot "see" neutrinos directly, they can study and monitor and track those tiny flashes of light.

As Qin got closer to the blue lab, she could see the site out on the snow where the neutrino researchers had drilled four holes into the ice sheet. Each hole was more than three thousand feet deep. Long strings of sensitive light detectors had been lowered down into the holes and frozen in place.

As neutrinos passed through the ice sheet, some of them would collide with atoms in the ice and create flashes of light. The light detectors would then pick up the telltale flashes and transmit data about each one back to computers in the blue lab. The researchers hoped that the data they collected about the flashes could be used to trace the paths of neutrinos back to their sources out in space.

Welcome warmth surrounded Qin as she stepped inside the air-lock entrance of the blue lab. She slipped off her parka and took off her thick insulated boots. Padding along in her socks, she made her way through a maze of instruments and computers to her work area at one end of the building.

She sat down at her desk and scanned the glowing computer screens on it. Beyond her desk loomed the massive computer system that was connected to the light detectors. It was constantly monitoring what was happening in the ice far below the surface.

They had run into a problem. At three thousand feet down, the ice was not as clear as the scientists had thought it would be. It was full of minute air bubbles. And the bubbles interfered with the way light flashes were detected. It was a problem that everyone involved in the project was trying to solve.

Qin typed in a command on a keyboard, and new readings

from a string of light detectors came up on one of the computer screens. She frowned. The numbers still didn't look right. For several weeks, she had been using the computers to test and adjust the light detectors that were buried deep in the ice, to see if the air bubble problem could somehow be solved from the surface. She wasn't having much luck.

It was beginning to look as if they would have to drill deeper into the ice sheet. The scientists had analyzed the ice down to five thousand feet below the surface. At that depth, it was almost bubble-free. New plans were being made to drill deeper holes and put in more light detectors. Until then, it looked like neutrinos were going to remain as elusive as they had always been.

Qin Sun checks the wiring of the huge computer system that monitors the neutrino detector.

About ten miles from the dome, Ellen Mosley-Thompson knelt in the snow next to a makeshift table. On the table was a section of an ice core, about three feet long, freshly cut from the polar ice sheet. Ellen peered closely at the perfectly shaped cylinder of ice. There were distinct layers in it. Each layer represented one year's snowfall.

Despite the fact that it was below zero, Ellen was wearing only thin plastic surgical gloves on her hands. Mittens and gloves were too bulky for what she was doing. And she couldn't use her bare hands because she didn't want to contaminate the core when she touched it. It needed to be handled with great

Ellen Mosley-Thompson cuts through one section of a core taken from the polar ice sheet.

care because it was more than just a piece of ice. It was a record of the past.

Working quickly but carefully, she slid the section of ice into a long plastic bag and stapled the open end shut. Then she eased the plastic-wrapped ice into a cardboard tube, labeled it, and laid it gently inside one of the specially made insulated boxes that were stacked on the snow behind her.

Ellen was packing up sections from one of six cores that she would be extracting from the ice sheet at the South Pole that season. She was an ice core paleoclimatologist from the Byrd Polar Research Center at Ohio State University. Paleoclimatologists use information gleaned from ice cores to piece together a picture of what earth's climate was like in the past.

"Here's number six!" said Bryan Mark, Ellen's field assistant, coming up with another slim cylinder of ice on a metal tray. He

Bryan Mark (right) *and a member of the drilling team ease the next piece of the core onto a metal tray.*

carefully set it down on the snow beside the table, next to sections 5 and 4.

"You guys are so efficient, you're getting ahead of me," Ellen said with a smile.

Bryan hurried back to help the two drillers on the next section. The coring rig that towered above the drillers chugged along steadily as it bored into the ice sheet. The core they were taking from this site would be sixty feet long.

Ellen looked past the coring operation at the white landscape that surrounded them. There was no building or person or landmark of any kind in sight. There was nothing but snow. It was not the sort of setting most people would find beautiful. But Ellen really liked it. And she loved the cold.

Ellen came around the table and picked up section 4. As she placed it on the table, she made sure that the top end of the core was on her left. It was critical to keep the sections in order and oriented correctly, top to bottom. When all of the sections were eventually laid out end to end, they would form a continuous record of the ice, with the youngest layers on the top and the oldest at the bottom. For the moment, Ellen was simply labeling and packing the sections, getting them ready for the trip home to her laboratory in Ohio.

It would be a long trip. When Ellen and the others had finished here, they would bury the boxes of core samples in the snow near the dome. At the end of the season—early in February—Ellen's cores would be flown to McMurdo and stored in a freezer. From McMurdo, they would be loaded onto a ship equipped with a special "cold room." The ship would sail from Antarctica to southern California, and from there the cores would be transported cross-country by refrigerated trucks. After a journey of more than ten thousand miles, the cores would finally be brought to the ice-core storage room at the Byrd Polar Research Center at Ohio State, ready for Ellen to begin analyzing them.

First, she would assign dates to each layer in the cores. Past events would make that job easier. Somewhere along each sixty-foot cylinder of ice, Ellen would find two layers that were radioactive—the result of fallout from the atmospheric testing of nuclear weapons in 1955 and 1964. Because the dates of the nuclear testing are known, an exact date can be assigned to the two radioactive layers. And once Ellen located those layers, the dates of the others would be easy to figure out.

After the layers in a core were dated, each one would be melted to determine its water content. That information, in turn, would be used to calculate how much snow fell that year in the area where the core was taken.

The information that Ellen extracts from her ice cores will make it possible for her to estimate how much snow has fallen at the South Pole every year for the last hundred years or so. She will be able to show how the annual snowfall has changed from year to year, and decade to decade, during the last century.

Why is this important? Many climate models suggest that precipitation rates will change worldwide as a result of global warming. Monitoring snow accumulation at the South Pole will help scientists check the accuracy of those predictions, adjusting the models if necessary, so that they will be able to predict with better accuracy potential climate change around the world.

Just inside the main entrance to the dome at the South Pole station there was a small orange building with BIOMED lettered on the door. Inside, Eileen Sverdrup, M.D., watched as

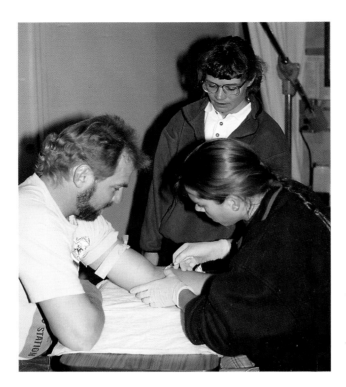

Eileen Sverdrup (back) *looks on while Katy McNitt practices drawing blood from a volunteer.*

Katy McNitt carefully inserted a needle into the arm of a friend who had volunteered to let her practice drawing blood from him. "Feel for the vein," instructed Eileen. "Swab it with alcohol. Keep the needle down, more parallel to his arm."

Eileen was the South Pole doctor. As the only professional medical person at the station, she was also dentist, X-ray technician, lab specialist, and counselor—all rolled into one. Unlike most of the people who were currently living and working at the station, Eileen would not be leaving when it closed down for the season. She and twenty-seven others, including Katy, would be staying behind to "winter-over."

When the South Pole station closes in early February each year, a small winter-over crew remains behind to keep the station running throughout the intense cold and perpetual darkness of the long Antarctic winter. In just a few weeks, Eileen and the other winter-overs would be entirely on their own. It would be nine months before they would see anyone from the outside world again.

Eileen was teaching Katy and a number of other people from the winter-over group how to stitch wounds, draw blood, and start IVs. Before the last plane of the season taxied down the runway and took off for McMurdo, she wanted to have a trained trauma team put together that could help her with a major medical emergency.

Every person who winters at the South Pole, or at any other Antarctic station, must pass very thorough medical exams. Eileen didn't expect that she'd be dealing with many diseases or common physical problems that winter. Her "patients" were all in excellent health. But anything could happen during the coming months of isolation—a fire, an explosion, some kind of accident. Eileen had to be prepared to deal with every possible medical problem, from burns and broken bones to major surgery or mental breakdowns. For nine months, she would have to make do with what she had in her operating room, lab, and drug cabinet, and with whatever help her trauma team could give her.

Eileen had left her medical practice in Fairbanks, Alaska, to take the job as South Pole doctor for a year. Spending the winter cut off from the rest of the world in one of the harshest environments imaginable was something she really wanted to do. Besides giving her experience in living and working in isolation, it was good medical training that forced her to be prepared for the unexpected. She also felt that her winter-over experience at the South Pole would be a big first step toward becoming a wilderness medicine specialist. She wanted to accompany explorers and scientists on expeditions into remote wilderness areas all over the world.

Katy withdrew the IV needle and put a bandage on her friend's arm. "That really helped, to run through it again," she said to Eileen, as they put away the equipment. "I think I'm starting to get the hang of it."

After the two "trainees" had left, Eileen straightened up the operating room and walked back to her small lab. BIOMED was not exactly like a modern medical clinic back in the United States. There wasn't much "high-tech" equipment around. Eileen's X-ray machine, for example, was an old-fashioned type with film that had to be developed by hand in a darkroom.

But in a place where everything had to be flown in by cargo plane and where spare parts could be delivered only during the brief summer season, the most up-to-date equipment wasn't necessarily the best choice. Everything Eileen used needed to be basic and reliable, easy to operate and easy to fix.

Just then a voice came booming over the loudspeakers in all the buildings under the dome. "We've got an incoming flight. Would the fuel team please report to the skiway immediately."

Eileen hurried to the entrance of BIOMED where a pair of insulated coveralls hung by the door. She pulled them on, shoved her feet into well-padded boots, and put on a face mask and goggles. She grabbed her hat and mittens and headed out the door. In addition to being the station's doctor, Eileen helped fuel planes. She also worked in the power plant now and then, and ran the mail room during the summer season.

Up on the skiway, she helped several other people drag thick rubber hoses to the edge of the landing field and then stood waiting in the bitter cold wind for the plane to arrive. They heard the droning of an LC-130 in the distance and then watched as it landed in a cloud of snow far down the skiway. A few minutes later, it taxied up in front of the dome.

The cargo team rushed over to the back of the plane to help unload boxes of supplies. Eileen dragged one of the hoses over to the plane's fuel tank, hooked it up, and signaled for the fuel to be turned on. All the while, the plane's engines kept running, its propellers roaring overhead. The pilots rarely shut down the engines when they landed at the South Pole. It was simply too cold. Once the engines were off, they usually wouldn't start again.

Passengers board an LC-130, ready to take off from the South Pole.

Auroras light up the dark polar night.

Later, as Eileen watched the big plane taxi down the skiway and take off into the pale blue sky, she wondered how she would feel the day the "last plane out" left for McMurdo, leaving the winter-over crew behind and alone.

Only a few people in the world have spent the winter at the South Pole. Eileen was looking forward to seeing the sun gradually set, placing a bet on when the temperature would first reach −100° F, and lying in the snow in the middle of the long Antarctic night, watching auroras light up the dark polar sky.

For Further Reading

Chipman, Elizabeth. *Women on the Ice: A History of Women in the Far South*. Melbourne: Melbourne University Press, 1986.

A detailed historical account, spanning the period from the early 1800s through 1984, of the women of many nations who have spent time in Antarctica. This book also discusses how attitudes have changed regarding the presence of women on the continent.

Darlington, Jennie. *My Antarctic Honeymoon: A Year at the Bottom of the World*. New York: Doubleday, 1956.

In 1947, Jennie Darlington and Edith "Jackie" Ronne joined their husbands and a group of other men on a year-long expedition to Stonington Island on the Antarctic Peninsula. Jennie and Edith were the first women to winter-over on the continent.

Johnson, Rebecca L. *Science on the Ice: An Antarctic Journal*. Minneapolis: Lerner Publications, 1995.

One woman's firsthand view of the lives and research of scientists who work in Antarctica.

Land, Barbara. *The New Explorers: Women in Antarctica*. New York: Dodd, 1981.

Stories about some of the first women who participated in the U.S. Antarctic Program during the 1970s.

Parfit, Michael. "Reclaiming a Lost Antarctic Base." *National Geographic Magazine* 183, no. 3 (March 1993): 110-126.

An article about East Base, a long-since-abandoned site along the Antarctic Peninsula. There the first two American women to live in Antarctica, Jackie Ronne and Jennie Darlington, spent 1947–1948 with their husbands and several other explorers.

Reader's Digest Editors. *Antarctica*. 2nd ed. New York: Reader's Digest Association, 1990.

An information-packed reference about Antarctica's geography, wildlife, climate, and much more, with detailed accounts of the people involved in the continent's discovery and exploration.

Index

About the Author

Rebecca L. Johnson has traveled to Antarctica twice on grants from the National Science Foundation. *Braving the Frozen Frontier* is the third book she has written based on her polar experiences. Her previous two Antarctic books are *Investigating the Ozone Hole* (1994 NSTA/CBC Outstanding Science Trade Book for Children) and *Science on the Ice: An Antarctic Journal* (1995 Scientific American Young Readers Book Award; 1996 NSTA/CBC Outstanding Science Trade Book for Children; Children's Literature Choice List). A native of South Dakota, Johnson grew up with prairie winters—experience that helped prepare her for Antarctica's often savage weather.

Rebecca L. Johnson (left) *and Bonnie Bratina collect soil samples on tiny Bratina Island—named for Bonnie's uncle.*

Photo Acknowledgments

The photographs have been reproduced with the permission of: Ann Hawthorne, pp. 1, 23, 29, 33, 44, 47, 56, 57, 59, 86, 88, 112; Galen Rowell / Mountain Light, pp. 2–3, 18, 19, 31, 40, 43, 78, 92, 95; Stuart Klipper, p. 8; © Stephen Schrader, pp. 10, 22, 107; Michael Castellini, pp. 12, 24, 35, 38, 54; © Rebecca L. Johnson, pp. 14, 16, 17, 32, 34, 50, 53 (both), 60, 64, 83, 84, 87, 89, 94, 96, 99, 100, 101, 104; Rich Kirchner, pp. 21, 46, 51, 62, 67, 71, 77; © Jody Forster, pp. 26, 42, 69, 80; Rob Jensen, p. 36; Gayle Dana, pp. 73, 74; Bert Davis, p. 75; Cheryl Hallam, p. 81; Bill McAfee, p. 108.

Front and back cover photos © Rebecca L. Johnson.